SHORT GAME

10 Scoring Zone Secrets to Mastering Golf from within 120 Yards

CONFIDENT
GOLFER

Copyright

Short Game – 10 Scoring Zone Secrets to Mastering Golf from Within 120 Yards

Copyright © 2016

http://www.confidentgolfer.com

Disclaimer

ISBN-13: 978-1517255381

ISBN-10: 1517255384

Table of Contents

You may also enjoy by Confident Golfer:

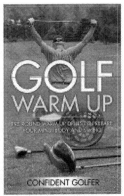

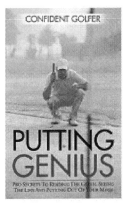

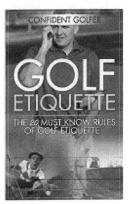

*** FREE GIFT ***

As a way of saying thanks I'd love to give you this AMAZING MIND HACK for GOLF. This is exclusively for readers of my books.

YOU WILL BE ABLE TO FOLLOW PROVEN STEPS USED TO GET IN THE RIGHT FRAME OF MIND BEFORE YOU HIT EVERY SHOT. DO NOT UNDERESTIMATE THE POWER OF A PRE-SHOT ROUTINE.

Visit the following link to download your **free copy** of

'GET IN THE ZONE'

www.confidentgolfer.com/getinthezone

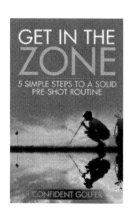

Foreword

Please allow me introduce you to Confident Golfer; however before I go into that I would like to tell you a real life story. When I was a 14 years old I can recall watching Nick Faldo win the British Open and after finding out that he started playing golf at the same age I decided that I was going to follow suit. At that time I had a pocket full of change and managed to buy a mix of used clubs from the local charity shop. Not one of them was made by the same company and to this day I have never seen or heard of those manufacturers again. But they suited me and just having the opportunity to play with them on a real golf course as opposed to playing pitch and putt at the local family run Par 3 6 hole course, was enough for me to fall in love with the game. Sadly, none of my family or friends played golf; therefore I had to get myself to and from the local club. I spent the next few years teaching myself (as we could not afford lessons) and subsequently engrained some pretty bad habits. The enthusiasm dried up and by the time I was 18 I was more interested in soccer and saving up to buy my first car than playing golf.

Fast forward some 15 or so years later to when I was 33 - I had a wife and child of my own and was earning a reasonable living. I had played the odd round of golf with my friends over the years but I decided at this point I was going to give golf a chance. I was going to see if I did have what it took to play at a high level. So, I came up with a plan and that plan was to turn pro by the time I was 50 so I could join the Seniors Tour. I figured that I had 17 years to do it. Armed with massive amounts of focus and determination I approached my local teaching pro and explained my goal. He felt it was absolutely possible and set about designing a plan that I could implement. We would regularly assess the progress and change the medium term goals, but to start off I needed a handicap.

As I said, I had only played a few rounds per year since I was 18 and had never officially been a member of a club, so that was the first step. Trying to rebuild a game after so long via lessons and getting a handicap was not easy; bearing in mind I had no friends or acquaintances that played golf. It took a number of weeks to find members who were prepared to mark three cards, but I managed it and started off with an official handicap of 24. The journey had begun. I disliked the members at that club so decided to move which proved to be the best decision I could have made. During the next five years I managed to do something that not many can say they achieved. I went from shooting in the high 90's to regularly shooting scores in the mid to low 70's.

You see, we keep hearing that although there are thousands of qualified PGA Teaching Professionals around the world the fact remains that the average handicap is not reducing. So what did I do that was different? What steps did I take to improve my overall game and ultimately my scores? Well, I did spend a lot of money and time on lessons. I also had some reality checks along the way and committed to numerous levels of improvement that I even surprised myself. I had full swing lessons, short game lessons, putting lessons – all with different coaches dedicated to a particular aspect of the golf swing. I had mind coaching and my clubs were custom fit a number of times. I dedicated myself to golf fitness, biomechanics feedback, spent time with amateur internationals and played numerous rounds of golf with Tour Pros. I read books, watched films and videos as well as purchased many improvement gadgets. I attended week long golf clinics overseas, not to mention spending hundreds of hours at the driving range and pitching balls in my back yard. I analysed the swings of the world's best players and the minds of the world's best sports men and women across a multitude of disciplines and I drew some interesting conclusions.

Now I am not a Professional Golfer, in fact a couple of years into my journey I realized that even if I did turn pro, I would I really want to be travelling the country or perhaps even Europe scrapping for a share of a small purse. Perhaps missing cuts and more importantly, missing my family. The reality did hit home and I changed my goals from becoming a touring pro to becoming the best golfer that I could be. What I learned in those few years taught me some outstanding and valuable lessons that I would love to share with my fellow Amateur golfer. Not the golfer that was not playing off a 5 handicap by the time they were 10 years old, having been introduced by a family member from an early age. Not the golfer whose natural athleticism was simply moulded by forging a repetitive swing from playing every week since they were a junior when the body was supple enough to be put under such pressure.

That was NOT me and I expect you are reading this book because that is probably not you either. It is the aim of Confident Golfer to talk to you from the heart, not as a PGA Professional, but as a regular guy who has been where every Amateur golfer has been. Make no mistake; the dedication and training I have invested in, is possibly unparalleled among the golfing fraternity. This quest for knowledge let me in fact to training and qualifying as a certified golf psychologist. You will find much of this approach comes across when reading any of my books. My knowledge of the technical, physical and mental aspects of the game has put me in a strong position to help the beginner, the mid handicap and equally the single figure golfer.

So if you are on a journey of improvement or if you simply want to gain some confidence on the tee, the fairway or the greens, then Confident Golfer will be perfect for you. It will take away a lot of the technical details and will simply allow you to just play the game. I am not a mind or a swing coach, but boy have I spent enough time with many of the industry's leading experts in these fields. I have worked out what I needed to do to better my all round game. In my business life I am an educator and manager of people and that is enough to help me know what people really need to hear. Many of my tips and suggestions will involve a golf instructor, but many of the principles I speak about will be things you have not heard of, things that anyone can do to simplify the game....I started late and won, I may have not turned pro, but I think I accomplished many things that not even the journeyman touring pro will ever achieve. I would love to share my journey with. Many of the principles are ones you will have heard of but the drills if done with commitment and focus really will help improve your scores.

I wish you so much success on the course and in your short game. As always I would love to hear from you at info@confidentgolfer.com and if you liked this book I would be so grateful if you left a review. Take care and keep swinging the club.

Introduction

Let me start off by asking you a question:

Would you rather be known as a player who can boom 300 yard drives straight down the middle of every fairway; or the golfer who can find most greens with a wedge from 120 yards? Now whilst this book will cover a lot more than this simple multiple choice question, I would like you to consider it for a moment nonetheless. Personally, I think most of us love the adoration of hearing the "oohs" and" ahhs" followed by the odd round of applause if we manage to stripe one off the tee. It's far more exhilarating than a muted "well done", should we manage to play a nice safe wedge to a fairly easy green. Wait a minute; I know the short game isn't as exciting as watching a ball flying 300 yards and staying on the fairway, however why is it that your handful of decent drives isn't good enough to beat the golfer that plots his way around the course. The same golfer that manages to get up and down from most areas of the course and regularly beats you with an unspectacular style of play?

I'll tell you why. It is because whilst you might be able to drive it well and perhaps even your wedge play is acceptable, the fact remains that your chipping and putting is probably not as good as it could be. Believe it or not your short game and more to the point your inability to get a handle on it are what contributes to the final number on your score card. It is not your ability to slam a drive 250 to 300 yards regularly.

Now I expect you are thinking to yourself "Well done Einstein, you have managed to write an introduction to a book which I have heard many times over and I even know the saying 'drive for show and putt for dough', so tell me something I don't know". Well ok, if you feel that way allow me to explain some simple and yet possibly forgotten basics.

Could it be that you have yet to find something you can apply to your personal game? Could it be that you are still looking for that Holy Grail or simple a shortcut to lower your handicap? Have you ever considered that perhaps you are not practicing the right things?

It may even be that you have never considered any of these ideas before but you have heard from a friend that the short game which is often referred to as the scoring zone is the place where you will save the most amounts of shots. If this is the case then you have come to the right place.

1. Importance of the Short Game

If you ask any elite golfer, (particularly tournament professionals) which area of the game is the most important to their scores and thus to their practice schedule, you will get the same answer 100 times out of 100 – The short game. They may break down their answers into various aspects of the short game, namely putting or wedge play; however the answer will encapsulate the same point.

Elite golfers are always in analysis mode when they are away from the course, asking questions of themselves such as: How many putts did I take, How many putts did I miss vs make? How many par scrambles did I convert? How many bunker saves did I make? And other questions that center on the four areas of the short game - being Putting, Chipping, Pitching and Bunker Shots.

If you as the Amatuer golfer are not prepared to ask pertinent questions of your short game, and then work on them, the simple fact remains that you will not see significant changes to your scores.

Taking time to study the areas of improvement specific to your game means you do not even have to pick up a club to get the inside edge on your buddy, competition or even just yourself. Taking time to think first and implementing a specific plan can be one of the best things you ever do to make significant changes to your scores.

So let's think for a moment about what percentage of your golf game is from 120 yards and in? Believe it or not it's 60 to 70 percent. So, doesn't that say something about the need to focus more on your short game than you long game? The answer is a simple Yes.

And so before we get to the bigger, finer detailed tips I would like to start by considering something.

Let's say you can only drive the ball 220 yards straight and true on a regular basis, but your short game, especially your putting needs work. Would it make sense to continue going to the driving range to keep ensuring your drives find every fairway? Why would you keep on practicing with your woods if it is a strong part of your game to the neglect of your short game?

A lot of it is to do with ego as we all like to get the driver out. After all , the fairway is typically a larger target and there is not as much pressure on us to achieve success in this area of golf compared to finding a small well-guarded green.

Now, I know you see a multitude of long game driving tips from the top instructors because that's where the money is for the golf teachers. But why would you keep on practicing your drives if you have a solid swing and ability to keep it on the fairway rather than hit the number of greens in regulation that would make a PGA pro feel a little nervous?

Like I said earlier the key to shaving strokes and improving your golf is to focus on your short game. What percentage you should be paying to wedge, pitch, and chip and putting shots is not a guessing game. You'll have to be a bit of a scientist and statistician of your game. What you'll want to do is literally do a survey and account for how well you're doing shot wise when hitting pitch, wedge, and chip shots as well as putts. Analyze things such as:

1. What percentage of putts am I sinking from certain distances?
2. With my pitch and wedge shots—can I get them on the green in a reasonable number of shots?
3. How many are missing the green completely and is there a pattern to the misses? Long, Short, Left or Right?

It may seem a dull task but if you want to take your game up a notch and beat your fellow golfers, you'll be determined to do these things. I personally used a piece of software call Scoresaver. It enabled me to note down the number of fairways hit, greens in regulation, missed greens and whether they were missed long, short, left or right. It showed me my total number of putts; par saves, getting up and down from bunkers, lost balls and much more. At the end of logging a round I was presented with a report of where I stood as a golfer and what areas I was deficient in. This was all extremely helpful data that I could use to make my practice sessions more productive.

There are certain things within the short game that you'll want to concentrate on because you may not be giving them the correct amount of attention. Of course, you need to keep practicing areas you do well in, but for now you'll need to focus on the weaker areas of your short game.

I realize I'm just generalizing here, but you need to appreciate that your focus has to be on your short game in order to get better as a total golfer. If you're a bit of a lab rat like me you'll enjoy finding out how well your short game is really doing. Even get the wife and the kids into it to take numbers to see where your game is strong compared to areas that need improvement.

It's easier than you think and I expect you'll enjoy the process and seeing the improvement in your short game.

If you could get the "real low down" on how to strengthen your short game and literally be given a blueprint that makes it easy to get better in a step by step approach that even the pros use, wouldn't it be worth it?

I think it would, and if PGA pros say that your short game is the key to getting better as a casual, good amateur or pro golfer, then it definitely would.

It is almost like getting results before you even pick up a golf club.

I honestly belief there lies a sharp shooter of a golfer in all of us if we just nail down the things that will help us take our short games to the next level. What are you waiting for? Now, whilst we touched on the statistical side, briefly read on as next we will consider some interesting statistics that will really get you thinking.

2. Understanding Short Game Statistics

In the world of sport there are so many statistics for the most mundane things it would make your head spin. Even in golf there are the odd stats that are of no value like how many 40 foot putts PGA players sink. Most golfers including pros don't sink them at all so there is no point talking about those kinds of statistics.

When I'm talking statistics that relate to the short game I don't mean how many putts you take per round and how many putts you take on the greens in regulation; I like to look at how far those putts are and how difficult they may be as well. Add to this the average distance from the hole your chips and pitches land, and you are suddenly armed with some helpful facts and figures to work with. This ultimately puts you in the best position to know what areas to focus on with your practice sessions.

However, before we get into statistics that relate to your own personal game I would like to share some research that I have been studying. We may not like to admit it but I think there is a scientist in all of us golfers; after all we constantly analyze our shots immediately after playing them along with the highs and lows of a round as soon as we get in the clubhouse. Consider the following data. It is gathered from hundreds of golfers who had their conversion rates of putts analyzed from different distances from the hole.

Distance from hole	% of putts made
2 feet	100%
3 feet	95%
4 feet	70%
6 feet	50%
10 feet	20%

What do you take away from the above figures? I think first and foremost it indicates that if you miss a green you are highly likely to secure at least a bogey if you cannot chip to within 4 feet. Now compare this to the following statistics taken from the default settings on the Scoresaver software I was talking about. It shows a statistical probability based on a golfers handicap level and I would tend to agree with it all:

Handicap	Fairways Hit	G.I.R	Putts	Sand Saves	Par Scrambles
28	16%	3%	40	5%	7%
24	24%	7%	38	7%	11%
20	32%	11%	36	9%	15%
16	40%	15%	34	10%	19%
12	48%	24%	33	14%	23%
8	56%	36%	31	21%	32%
4	63%	48%	30	35%	44%
0	71%	64%	29	55%	60%

Whilst this is not going to apply in every case, you can see

21

that as the handicap level reduces all the statistics improve.

However, it is a fact that as you get closer to the green, your chances of getting yourself out of trouble vastly reduce because simply put you are running out of shots to use to improve on a bad mistake. What do I mean by that?

Well let's compare two golfers. The first golfer plays to a handicap of 28, and according to the statistics is expected to miss most greens in regulation. In order for this to be a reality the chances are, according to the "statistics" that they will take one more shot to get to every green which isn't unreasonable to assume for a beginner golfer. We can also see that shots are lost by taking a number of three-putts.

The second golfer plays to a handicap of 8. Even though he too misses greens he does manage to average 13 Greens in Regulation. An 8 handicapper will not often 3-putt and even though they find more fairways which you would think is the reason they find more greens in regulation; the interesting statistic for me in the Par Scrambles. This is borne out by the fact that if you take the scratch golfers figures, they save par 60% of the time. And this is the golden nugget that you can take from statistics. EVERY GOLFER WILL MISS A GREEN. But it is their ability to still turn a double bogey into a bogey or a bogey into a par that contributes to a reduced handicap. And this comes from having a better than average short game. I hope this makes sense.

To reduce our handicap we cannot just assume that we will be able to hit the ball further or even find more fairways because as we all know a fairway found offers absolutely no guarantee that we will find the green. Anyway, being able to get stronger and longer off the tee may not be an option depending on our age or physical health. In the past, I have personally been in the middle of the fairway happy as you like and then proceeded to shank the ball, under hit it, or snap hook it out of bounds. Of course I'd always rather be on the fairway, however there have been many occasions where I have still found the green from a nasty lie in the rough after a bad tee shot.

Still need convincing? I'd like to paint a picture on a 505 yard par 5. Now, we know we can only control ourselves in golf and at times even that seems difficult. The following scenario could be one of many possible outcomes. However, see what you think.

Shot 1:   3 Wood that slices in the wind and tumbles into the rough at about 200 yards and comes to rest behind a tree.

Shot 2: Hacked 7 iron which advances no more than 120 yards but is on the fairway. You are left with 185 yards to a green well-guarded by bunkers and water to either side. Either way it will take the best 4 iron you can hit to find the heart of the green but you decide the risk is too great.

Shot 3: You take a 5 iron which doesn't come off as you intended and travels 165 yards. You are now left 20 yards short of the green which isn't so bad, so what do you do? Your choices are, play it safe and go for bogey and accept if that's how you are playing that you will score around 18 over par for the day. Or you do something else.

You implement the short game tips in this book and give yourself a much better chance of getting up and down and securing par. After all it was stoke index 1, therefore it's technically the easiest hole to play on the course and all that has happened is you have played the hole badly up until this point. But this doesn't mean you have to accept bogey or more. Until the ball is in the hole you have a chance to influence the total amount of shots played and as Walter Hagen used to say 3 bad shots and 1 good one still makes par.

Now think about this, if you understand and know your short game statistics, and especially putting ones, you'll know you need to focus to make your short game better.

Would you agree?

Well, I hope so and if you would like to know how the statistics really affect your short game then read on.

Pitch, Wedge and Chip Shot Statistics

These shots are in the short game realm and knowing the number of shots you play in your approach to the green is vital as well. Your Wedge shots and Putting stokes are possibly the keys to supreme success on the course. But knowing your numbers can tell you what you need to do short game wise.

What you want to really know is you're putting stats from certain distances. You need to know your wedge and pitch shot numbers from certain yardages.

Putting Statistics

The other statistic you want to measure is when you're putting. How successful is your putting from certain distances. This is my favorite stat. Measure your success rate from certain distances in most practice sessions. Remember the chart on page 19.

Wedge Statistics

Now here's a short game tip that not many golfers use or even know about. It's to do with wedge and pitch shots.

1. Hit about 10 shots making sure to measure their distance from the hole before you play.
2. Measure how far each shot went and their distance away from the hole.
3. Add up how far the 10 shots went and divide that number by 10.

That will tell you your average distance away from the hole. This is not exact science other than that math never lies. Next, you want to do the following

1. Figure out how the math plays out as far as what types of lie on the fairway you are hitting it from and how close to the hole you are hitting it.
2. And on the average how far from the pin you're landing it.

Even take notes on how you approached certain lies, fairways or greens and the success ratio. That is another tip so if you run into an issue off the fairway, in a bunker or a pitch area just below the fairway, you'll know how to approach that shot in the future.

What you want to do is get a handle on your approach

shots. Meaning, what do you usually do at a certain point on the fairway after hitting a drive? Yes, I'm including driving in here.

All of this math will also help in determining how close you need to hit your wedge and pitch shots and make those key putts.

Just by knowing your own statistics for distance and number of shots played will not help you putt better, but it will help you get closer to the hole if you take action and actually practice regularly to bring your scores down because you know how to shoot from certain distances or positions.

To get an even better handle on your stats and how far you're hitting wedge, pitch or putt shots get a tape measure, or even better get an App or GPS device that will measure the distance you're shooting from.

Knowing how often you're sinking putts and reaching certain distances to the green will also help your game and help you approach it like a scientist and a sports scout. That's what golf is to some degree, all about numbers. But practice is also key to that entire math process.

Also, knowing which shots give you the best chance of

success and ones that won't, will keep you focused on improving aspects of your game that will make you better. And all this because you simply took a little time to analyze the impact of short game statistics and how they relate to your own numbers and metrics so to speak.

Now the next chapter is perhaps the most important and whilst you may have heard some of the information before I offer my own personal insight based on some specific research.

3. The Secret of 120 Yards

I think that the 150 yard marker is a comfort blanket to most of us. It's the one yardage marker where we begin to feel happy and in control of our game. Ever since we started playing golf, the one club that we used for lessons, range practice and even the local pitch and putt course was the trusty 7 iron and for the majority of us that is our 'go to' club for playing shots from 150 yards.

So then, shouldn't we be talking about the secret of 150 yards? What is this secret of 120 all about?

Well, I have spent a lot of time studying this and here are my conclusions.

I conducted a study of 100 amateur golfers. I asked them two questions:

1. What is your favorite distance to the green?
2. What is your favorite club?

I waited for the answer to the first question before I asked the second question and for good reason.

I did not want them to link the two. For example, when

answering question one many said 150 yards but then answered question two by saying their Pitching Wedge was the club they felt most comfortable with.

Out of 100 people I interviewed many said 150 yards to question number one which resonates with the thoughts mentioned at the beginning of this chapter, whilst other said 100 yards. These were the 2 distances that came up the most, but interestingly when I asked the second question the majority of people said the Pitching Wedge.

After I had this discussion I then asked the first question again and the results were interesting as the answers ranged from 130 – 110 yards which from the golfers I interviewed was the average distance they hit their Pitching Wedge.

What can we learn from this? To me it spells out the fact that if we could get our approach shots to a distance of around 120 yards we would likely see more pars and even more birdies. Of course this study is not conclusive and it very much depends on which set of golfers you are interviewing, however for me it provided interesting feedback.

Knowing What Clubs to Use from 120 Yards: The Secret—Well Not Really a Secret

Before you even think of heading out on to the course, head over to the driving range to establish how far you are hitting your clubs on that particular day. Reason being that if you're out on the course and fumbling in your bag to choose the right Iron or Wood, you are wasting time and the chances are if you don't know what club you need in your bag to hit shots from 120 yards you are going to struggle?

Whilst we are talking about this I would apply this tip to all of your clubs. Write down how far you're hitting the ball using different irons and use that for future reference on the course. I made a chart which I laminated and put in my scorecard holder. You may wish to do the same. At the very least keep tabs on how far you hit each iron or wood. That way you'll know exactly what you're dealing with, and not just guessing what to use. I call it the Golf Game Scouting Report. You will need to use this in different weather conditions too.

It will be one of the keys to your game.

Oh, before you head out on the course get a handle on how far you can hit your wedge and pitch clubs too. I will

31

expand on this more in chapter 6.

How to Play Difficult Shots from 120 Yards

There are a number of shots which you may not often need to play depending on which course you are at. However you are bound to play them at some point and it is good to look for ways to practice these are the range or even out on the course if time allows. Here we have outlined four of the more common difficult shot and how to approach them:

The Down Slope Shot

These in my estimation are one of the toughest shots to play. When you're dealing with a downhill slope you want to first of all center your body so that your shoulders are parallel to the slope itself. You will find that most of your weight in now on the lead foot.

1. Place club head behind the ball and position your feet slightly wide that normal to increase your stability on the slope you are playing from.
2. The ball should be slightly in front of the middle of the stance. If the slope is very steep it is easy to hit the ground before the ball, therefore position the ball further back in your stance where it is easier to

make clean contact with the ball first.

3. Once you have set up, lower your left shoulder until parallel with the slope. From this position your swing will travel with the slope and make clean contact with the ball rather than hitting into the slope behind it. Leaning your shoulders into the slope puts more weight on your left foot – about 60%

4. Because of the slope the majority of your weight will stay on your lead foot during the back and down swing. Remember the slope will cause the ball to come off the club face lower than normal so take this into consideration when choosing your club. You may need to take one less club. The ball tends to fly to the right on a downhill slope because having more of your weight on the left foot makes it easy to end up with your body ahead of the ball on impact so be careful with your weight transition.

With shots like a down slope, experiment with both pitch and wedge clubs. You might do better with a different club than the normal choice when it comes to 120 yards and in.

The Sand Trap:

Probably the worst place to be from 120 yards is a fairway bunker. This is tough for a lot of players as well. But I'll make this simple. Keep more of an upright stance because you're going up, not down. Keep your lower body still and use just your arms more and swing past your body for a more solid swing. This way you'll hit the ball more solidly out of the sand trap or bunker.

The Rough And How To Approach It Like A Pro:

The part of the course where the grass pretty much does what it likes is even tougher to play a good shot from than when you are in a sand trap. A shot from the rough is somewhat deceptive because even though it's in a denser patch of turf it can run on farther due to there being hardly any back spin placed on the ball which is caused by blades of grass getting between the club face and ball.

Keeping your lead wrist firm through the impact of your swing and keeping an accurate swing that hits the ball between the toe and heel of the club head, will drive the ball through impact more effectively. As well, playing this shot with the club head face open more, will help drive the ball farther.

Okay, last tip on 120 yard scenarios:

Playing a Bare Lie:

What you will need to do when you play from a bare lie with a pitching wedge is always to hit the ball first, especially when the turf is harder. You always tend to end up getting a divot of grass, sand, dirt etc. Now, here's a good way to approach this shot.

Once you have taken your stance keep a little pressure on your front foot and slightly bring the shaft forward. Now take your backswing and focus on hitting the ball first. Focus on your front foot and wrist, keeping them firm and swing through. For lies that have softer turf you'll want to keep the same type of shot approach.

4. What the Pros Practice the Most and Why

Why do people do the things they do, especially when it comes to a PGA tour player?

Well, mainly because it works and it's been going on for many decades. For most players they unfortunately focus on the wrong aspects of their game and continue to flounder.

It's not about having god given talent. If that were the case, there would be about 10 guys on the tour. Most of the success you will get in your short game is purely work and effort driven, which means practicing in order to stay on that treadmill to success.

Now since the short game is the most important part of success for a pro and as we have established even the amateur golfer, it would be a good idea to commit the majority of practice time to it. That means at least 60% I would say.

Why? Because the majority of an amateur golfer mistakes come from wedge, pitch and putt shots. That's where your flaws will show the most.

The specific areas of your short game that you should

focus on is another thing altogether.

Let's break them down individually.

Putting

Putting can be classed at the most important part of your game. To me it is, and I personally think you should focus on it as well. Too many players never even practice two footers regularly and wonder why they miss easy putts. Here is a good guide to follow to improve your putting:

1. Start off with 10 x 2 foot putts.
2. Then 10 x 3 foot, 4 foot and 5 foot putts. This seems like a lot of work and it is. But if you want to be better, put in the work. By being able to sink 3 to 5 foot putts 80% of the time will help you with your longer ones.
3. Work hard on the short putts and start slowly introducing the 7 to 10 footers.
4. Move to 20 feet, hitting 10 of each.

This is simple but harder than it sounds. But please trust me because being solid on the greens will result in a great deal of success.

Oh, by working on the short and long putting together will

help the long lag putts get closer so you're not always fighting against par.

Ok, now onto the area of the course around the green, that being chipping and pitching.

Pitching:

The PGA Tour Pros have their issues with pitch shots just like you and I do. They take action to deal with them though, so let's take a look for a moment at what they do.

One of the greatest short game players on tour is Zach Johnson. When he won the US Masters in 2007 he didn't reach any of the par 5's in two shots at all, but was able to rely on a sharp short game and his pitching was on fire which led to birdie after birdie. One simple tip that he used was to keep the wrists set when swinging the club back and through. He didn't break the wrists at all. He used the 'V' created by his arms from the shoulders to the hands and kept that going through to the club head. Try it yourself. What you want to do is connect both lower and upper body when doing pitch shots. This way you'll have shots that stay on line more effectively.

Don't use your lower body to the detriment of your upper

body. As well, keep in mind you're not putting so don't use your hands so much. Make the force of your pitch about the body, not your hands. Here is an image of the follow through to help you visualize. See the 'Y' formed by the arms and club shaft after impact

:

Visualizing and making a mind body connection, especially your mind and upper body being key, will provide better success when pitching and getting to your target in fewer strokes.

One more thing is to keep a good check on your back swing and where your hands are in relation to ball positioning. If you have to use too much back swing your pitch shots tend to have too much loft and often slice and veer off to the left and right of the green.

But one thing I want you to remember about pitch and wedge shots is that they can be the catalyst to getting you to the green faster, but I implore you to practice these shots like crazy in your short game!

These are probably the toughest shots besides your putting. They will make you or break your game.

Here is what to do. Keep the club face open and then put a two handed grip on your wedge club. That way you will be positioned better. Then take your club back and get hinged wrist action going. That way when you swing your stroke won't be off line. If you follow through on the swing and your right hand stays below your left, the ball will stay elevated enough and stay on a more aligned path to your target.

Stay committed to swinging through impact. That way you don't increase spin on the ball. Putts are like that to some degree. Think about baseball pitchers who put a lot of spin on the ball. Chances are they are pitching changeups, curve balls or knuckle balls. All pitches with a lot of spin on them. You don't want that.

Bunkers:

Part of a Tour Pro's warmup before a major tournament undoubtedly will include splashing shots out from the bunker. This is paramount to them developing a sharp short game. Not one professional golfer can avoid bunkers and the harder the course the more strategically placed bunkers will be and yes this applies to amateurs too. The bunker is a place where I have seen so many amateurs lose it completely and we will come to the way to approach a bunker in the next chapter, however let me conclude by saying that I spent a whole day watching tour pros back in 2012 play bunker shot after bunker shot and I was surprised at the ratio of balls that they managed to land within 5 feet. I mean honestly, a pro is looking to hole out from everyone around the green INCLUDING a bunker and guess what, every now and again they do. What does that tell you?

To me it highlights the fact that we need to regard a bunker as just another area on the course. Forget that it's a trap. Most amateurs are not looking to get the ball up and down from a bunker, let alone in for a birdie, but stop and think for a moment....there is no reason why you cannot get it close. Good course management will dictate on occasion that you swallow your medicine from a bunker as you may have to play out sideways or even backwards which is another story altogether. However, if you approach a bunker in the same way mentally as a pro does you are half way there.

In conclusion, practicing your short game will undoubtedly make your game better. It works for the pros and it can work for you. I watched practice day at the Arnold Palmer Invitational at Bayhill Golf Club in 2013 and was amazed at how long they spent at the chipping and putting greens compared to the driving range. There is a real lesson there.

5 Wedge Shots That Are Key to Success

Now closely linked to looking at the things we see the pros do is the amount of attention they not only dedicate to the short game but the different kind of shots they are able to do with their short irons. It's funny because I've always thought that putting and short putting were more important than wedge, pitch and driving shots. But I'm starting to come around to the conclusion that practicing your wedge shots is just important as any other aspect of your short game.

And there are a number of wedge shots you have to understand as well. I know that most will not enjoy practicing, especially wedge shots, but like I said before it's the uninteresting stuff in golf that will help your game.

This may all seem a little much but it's all relevant to wedge shots. In my opinion there are five types of wedge shots you need to get hold of:

The Lob Wedge Shot

This has often been referred to as the 'flop shot' and it's a shot that high handicappers fear and usually for good reason. The lob shot requires you to play a high shot over an obstacle such as a bunker and get the ball to come to rest almost immediately. The problem with this is that due to the loft of the club which in most cases is around 60-64 degrees you cannot tickle the ball otherwise nine times out of ten it will land straight it he hazard you are trying to avoid. This introduces fear number two – playing with the amount of force you would usually use to hit the ball 50+ yards but this time you only need to hit it say 10 yards. You need to be making clean contact with the ball. It's a brushing motion where we clip the ball off the turf and are not looking to take a divot.

If you do not make clean contact with a lob wedge, typically the ball it will travel about 50 yards straight along the floor and possibly nearly kill our playing partners waiting patiently on the green a few yards away. These are not easy shots, but equally they do not have to be hard either and I'm here to make that process a little easier because my lob wedge is my favorite club. Having said that the only time you want to use this shot is when you're in precarious position, and no other club will do. When you're dealing with these shots you need a good lie or it gets inevitably tougher. A good lie will make the lob wedge shot easier.

This is what you will need to do:

1. Take your lob wedge and position your body so that the ball is just a bit forward of the center of your stance.
2. Your feet should be quite close together and angled a little towards your target.
3. You need to keep your shoulders square to the target.
4. Your weight should be distributed evenly to both feet.
5. Due to the ball position, your hands will not be as far forward as with the chip shot but still they will be slightly ahead of the ball.
6. The shaft will be slightly upright
7. Grip down the club so that your left hand is about 2-3 inches from the top of the club
8. DO NOT have the ball too far forward you ARE NOT

trying to scoop at it. Equally not too far back which leads to a low ball flight as they club head is still descending when it makes contact with the ball.

9. You will need to open the face depending on how high and steep you wish the ball to land as typically even a 60 degree lob wedge will have some roll on landing. Practice using different levels of open face to see how they react.

10. This is not a wristy swing. Simply make a back swing transferring the weight to your back foot and turn your arms at the same time. As you swing through, transfer your weight to your lead leg. DO NOT SWAY, as we are looking for a nice turn, back and through. Keep you left arm moving.

11. Do not allow the right arm to dominate as this will cause the back of the left write to collapse ruining any chance of clean contact with the correct angle of the club face.

12. Now make sure to keep the club head opened. Once again keep your lead hand on top of your follow through and bring your swing through so that your bottom hand ends up higher than your lead hand through impact with the ball.

13. With every Lob Wedge shot, practice and visualize the ball flight and feel the kind of swing required to land the ball where you need. Remember you are not aiming to hole it necessarily so allow some

freedom to give yourself a nice putt for par rather than play to land to a 5" landing spot to nail the shot.

That in a nutshell is the lob shot and although you will be using your lob wedge to play full shots of around 50-60 yards the finesse 'up and over' is a delight to be able to master, so get practicing. Now we move onto the good old pitch and run shot.

The Pitch and Run Shot

Unlike the lob shot, the pitch and run is probably the easiest wedge shot to play. This is done on more of a flatter part of a fairway. Notice I said fairway. This is not the same at greenside wedges which we will cover next. Like with all wedge shots and in fact irons throughout the bag, the importance of making contact with the ball first is absolutely necessary. Golfers that play to a decent level are aware that a divot is a good thing under the right circumstances, but more importantly a divot AFTER the ball is what you want to see, not a crater before the ball.

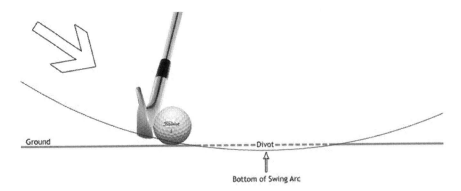

Ground

Divot

Bottom of Swing Arc

We are not looking to help it on its way by landscaping the fairway in the hope that the turf we hit sends the ball on its merry way. Saying that, a divot is not always necessary it's just that if we need to create a divot its always after we have struck the ball because it shows that we have crunched down on the ball with the face of the club. Using (hopefully clean) grooves to react with the dimples provides that lovely biting action from the ball as it stops almost immediately after landing. It's not rocket science and although we all marvel when we witness that result we are all in fact capable doing it.

This is what you will need to do:

1.   Position the ball to the right of center encouraging clean contact between ball and club face. You may want to play the ball even further towards your back foot to encourage the club to make contact with the ball on a descending strike. Notice the ball position

here is further back in the golfer's stance.

2. Once again bring back the wedge to about halfway and then using the body and arms to rotate bring your club forward and use your body to power the ball through the ball. This is actually more of a grunt shot that you need to use the power of your body like a power lifter does when powering through a maximum weight. And keep your body positioned once again toward your target.

3. You can even use an iron—a 9 iron on this shot if you like, but a medium loft wedge will do the trick.

4. Like with the lob wedge lead with the left arm (if you are right handed) and keep the hands moving slightly

ahead of the club head through impact.

Your aim with this relatively simple shot it to get the ball rolling as soon as possible. Whether you choose to do this using the contours of the fairway for good old links golf is up to you. **You can also see in our image the golfers feet are close together which encourages good balance.**

Chip and Run Shot:

This is an interesting wedge shot played from close to the green. It is much like the pitch and run shot although depending on the position of the flag in relation to where you are and the amount of fringe grass you need to carry it will require a degree of finesse and feel. You will be looking to get the ball rolling as soon as possible so there is no need to be a hero. Unless there is a huge puddle in the green between you and the flag then the log shot is out of the equation. So how do you play the chip and run. Well it is not dissimilar to a putt really

This is what you will need to do:

1. Take a narrow stance
2. Ball in center of stance
3. Now turn both feet to the left. The ball will look like it is now positioned more toward the back foot. This will

also encourage weight to be distributed to lead foot at a 60/40 ratio.

4. Club shaft is centered

5. Drop the left shoulder forward only slightly which encourages a descending blow on the ball. This is better than pressing the hands forward.

6. Leading with hands swing back and through with a club that will get the ball rolling as soon as possible. Consider the following as a guide as to which club will produce the amount of roll required depending on how close you are to the flag:

Flight to Roll Ratio	
GW	1:1
PW	1:2
9 Iron	1:3
8 Iron	1:4
7 Iron	1:5

What does this all mean? In essence, it shows that if you play a Gap Wedge and it spends 5 yards in the air it will travel 5 yards when it lands on the green. Much of this depends on the stimp reading but the above would in most cases apply if you are playing on a level green. But it also means you need to practice a lot around the chipping green to see what reactions you get from different distances. We can illustrate it this way:

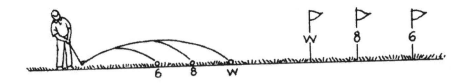

Other factors that will affect the ball flight, roll and final outcome are the grain and depth of the rough or fringe you are playing from. You also need to ensure the balls you are practicing with are those that you will use on the course and if you play on different courses I would suggested making this routine part of you pre-round warm up so that you get a feel for the type of greens you will be playing on for that particular day.

I would not normally advocate this tip, however when all else fails many golfers will say you have to do what feels natural and whatever it takes to get the ball in the hole. With this in mind you can always go ahead and use a putter. I'm not kidding. If you're not good with pop up shots with a wedge or iron, roll the ball with a putter. Once again, use a short stance and a short compact swing. This is a great alternative for the fringe of the green, however depending on the amount of fringe to play through and the moisture you may struggle to judge the distance effectively.

Wedge Shots from the rough:

When the ball is sitting down in the grass, I see golfers tend to chop down into it and the club just digs down and gets caught up in the grass. So there are a few things to do with this kind of shot.

1. Take a Sand or Lob Wedge and you need to learn to get the bottom or bounce of the club to work though the ground. This will cause the club to slide though the grass which will not allow it to grab the club head.

2. You need to take a long enough swing so the club can drop and get some momentum to get through the grass. If you use a short swing you will not be giving the club a chance to get through the thick grass. So it's important to use enough of a swing with the correct acceleration to get the ball out. Tom Kite used a simple rule that if he was in deep rough 30 yards from the flag he would play the swing that he would use to hit the ball 50-60 yards under normal conditions. Sounds simple enough.

3. As the club drops you need to keep the body rotating.

4. Stay relaxed with the arms so the club has enough swing. Then when it makes contact with the ball it will not shoot off the club face. Remember too that if the rough is particularly thick and dense you will need to give strength to your wrists without strangling the

grip too tight. Practice is required for this, particularly if you're green keeper is a fan of lots of rough on his course.

The Sand Trap Explosion Shot:

I always love seeing wedge shots like these in pictures and in slow motion video on the golf channel. Yes, I'm repeating aspects of this course, but if I didn't then you wouldn't understand how to work on the various aspects of my advice on the short game. You wouldn't take action and get better as a confident wedge shot player. I want you to succeed. Okay, back to the sand trap explosion shot.

This is one wedge shot you want get over the lip and onto the green with a full swing. Using your sand or lob wedge for this one open your club head face just opposite your lead foot. Take your stance and dig in for stability. Don't angle your shaft or risk the shot veering off where you don't want it to go. You are looking to open your stance slightly so that your body is open to the target. This means that your feet and body aim left and your club face aims right or straight at the flag. (See image)

Hit under the ball with a 3 quarter swing and power through the sand. By aiming to hit the sand 2–3 inches before the ball you create that explosion of sand that brings the ball out contained in the sand you hit.

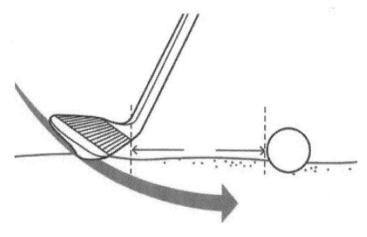

To get more lift in your shot and get it more on target,

keep leading with the front foot, but bring your hands through the swing and slightly pivot your back and front leg at the same time, keeping your shot in line with your front leg. Then just follow straight through with your turn ensuring you form a complete swing with the arms.

When you can complete this exercise you will see the ball is overtaken by the club head and it is powering through the sand. SO many golfer think that they must hot the ball first and if they are near the flag then the most definitely must not hit the ball hard. The fact remains that you are not hitting the ball. You are hitting the sand which forces the ball out of the bunker. This in turn with the motion carries the ball out softly. It also means you can hit the sand hard with a full swing. See image below and note that the club head has travelled past the ball.

** WEDGE BONUS TIP **

You may have heard this before, especially if like me you are a massive advocate of statistics. It's the concept of 12 shots with 4 clubs. This is something I do with all four of my wedges. I use a PW and 52, 56 & 60 degree wedges.

It involves taping or sticking to the shafts (near the grip) a guide for how far you hit each wedge using a 7:30pm, 9:00pm and 10:30pm back swing. If you practice this enough you will have three distances per club that you can rely on and have a total of 12 yardages to use when you are anywhere from 10-120 yards out from the green. I cannot tell you how much confidence this has brought to my game and I urge you to try it also and I am confident you will see similar results.

Yards	Club	Swing
40	60°	7:30pm
50	56°	7:30pm
55	60°	9:00pm
60	52°	7:30pm
70	PW	9:00pm
75	56°	9:00pm
85	52°	9:00pm
90	56°	10:30pm
95	PW	9:00pm
100	52°	10:30pm
110	PW	10:30pm

Notice how I have a distance from 40 to 110 yards that I can play to within 5 yards with all of my wedges. This tip helped me more than you can imagine with practice.

5. Never Fear a Bunker Again

Whilst we are on the subject of bunkers, I think it would be a good time to talk about them in a little more detail. We want to consider greenside bunkers as well as the bunkers you find anywhere from 30 – 120 yards out from the green. Ask any tour pro most of them would say that they prefer to be in a greenside bunker than the deep rough. This is because they feel they can get more control of the ball and introduce spin without even touching the ball itself which sounds strange I guess. On the other hand most amateur golfers seem to think that sand trap shots mean taking half swings and literally just barely touching the ball to get it out. Particularly around the green when you are so close to the flag. I mean, honestly why would you take a full swing when you are a few feet from the hole. It happens to the best of players and having an approach to these shots that you strategize on which not only gets you out of the bunker, but in a great spot on the course for your next shot or in the case of a greenside bunker – right by the flag is a tool you need to have in your bag.

It's not just important to think about that initial sand trap shot, but to think about where you want it to land so that it's in a spot that gives you leverage. Hard shots are part of the game, but being able to limit those can mean saving strokes and having a strong short game.

Wanting to know the real tips on your short game will keep you ahead in your game and ahead of even the local golf pro believe it or not.

Greenside Bunker Shots:

Okay, first figure out how far you are from the hole. Because if it is close you want that shot to be a bit shorter than usual. What you'll want to do if it's a short bunker shot to the hole is the following:

1.   Get yourself settled into the sand. This will not only get you grounded but give you a feel for the type of sand you are playing from. Ensure your stance is open to the target slightly.

2.   Notice how the shoulders, hips and feet are parallel

with the slope in this illustration.

3. Keep the ball further ahead in your stance near the front foot.

4. Open your club face toward your target.

5. Ensure the shaft is almost pointing backwards towards your right shoulder meaning a nice entry into the sand before just the ball by 2 inches or so.

6. Make a full swing and keep swinging through and as you make contact with the sand get the club face pointing towards the sky as soon as possible. (See image and note that even though there is a full swing the ball is still only a few yards from the golfer)

30 – 120 Yard Bunker Shots:

Many would agree that from this range you would be happy to just get the ball out of the trap and back into play. However, it doesn't have to be this way and I want to talk about a simple way to address this kind of shot.

In order to do this effectively we need to break this distance bunker shot down even further.

30 – 70 Yards

70 – 120 Yards

From 30-70 yards I have found that using my same green side bunker strategy is perfectly acceptable. The only thing I would do differently is to club down bearing in mind I am looking to take the sand out along with the ball. For example I would replace Pitching Wedge with a 9 Iron to compensate for the sand. Try this but remember to commit to the shot.

From 70–120 yards it becomes a little easier believe it or not. From this distance you are looking to play a typical fairway bunker shot where you would be looking to make contact with the ball first and nip it off the sand. It won't overshoot your intended target either. Having said that you still need to have a good stroke on the ball, but limiting it to about a three quarter swing will save you from those nasty extra strokes that humble even the best players.

1. Take a fairway stance in the sand and play the ball as you would if you were on the fairway.
2. Ensure you are comfortable with your stance and stability in the sand.
3. Take a swing with ¾ power and ¾ length.

Many golfers have issues with bunker or sand trap shots. You'll want to spend time practicing and getting comfortable with these shots. Remember too, that depending on the type of bunker you will need to compensate and remind yourself that you are not just hitting the sand or taking too full a swing. If you can practice in a variety of situations you will become confident in playing those bunker shots.

There are differing schools of thought out there and I've read articles where experts say you should hit the sand

and not the ball. For me it's simple.

- If you are playing a fairway bunker you hit the bal.
- And if you are playing a greenside bunker shot you hit the sand and allow the ball to pop out with the sand.

There will be limited contact for a greenside bunker shot and it's that which causes the ball to come to rest almost immediately after landing on the putting surface. You still need a good follow through and to keep your swing either full or partial in order to transfer the required motion, energy and forward movement into the sand to get the ball out.

Keeping in mind all this will keep your bunker shot strategy on target. I know many of you will hate taking notes or having a plan and you just want to enjoy playing golf. But for those who want to play at an advanced level as a local amateur or have visions of being on the PGA tour, take notes and apply these strategies in your sand trap shots and other aspects of your short game.

This way you'll always be moving ahead in both your short game and yes, you're driving too.

6. How to Avoid Missing Greens

I hope you have been able to put the book down and find time to implement a few of these tips on the short game and are taking action. Remember what was said about getting your results in advance? Little steps are nevertheless still steps forward.

This next chapter talks about another aspect of golf that mystifies even the top pros - How not to miss greens. Why would we talk about this when even the top pros miss greens? And if you watch the golf channel enough you will see plenty of golf balls go flying over a green with the commentator uttering "that's another missed green". So you can see that it happens even to the best of them.

It hurts, but we're here to help you stop missing the green so much. It's not just about making greens in regulation like the pros, and that's a great goal, but we're here to help you with strategies to help you be more confident in your approach shots to the green. Period.

Let's get you started on making better approach shots to the green, resulting in fewer missed greens.

Accurate Shots versus Distance

When you're out about 100 to 200 yards out from the green what do you think is more important - distance or accuracy? Well I guess that depends on the level of inaccuracy. For me I would prefer to sacrifice distance than be out of bounds, in the water, plugged in a greenside trap, or behind a tree. However, if your definition of inaccuracy was to miss a green by a few feet or yards, whilst still maintaining your desired distance then I am sure you would be equally as happy because then we simply have to work on our chipping and putting.

There are 2 main approaches to not missing greens constantly.

1. Knowing what clubs are best for certain distance's
2. How to play the ball from 100 to 120 yards so the ball stays on your target: The Green

Club Selection: If you're 100 to 120 yards out from the green it pays to know what club is best to use. It is also important to know if the ball will stay on the green in that one shot. So you will need to know if the green runs fast or slow. That's when club selection is paramount to getting the ball safely on the green.

Ask yourself, how will the ball react when it gets to the green?

If the green is fast you want to club down and aim for the front part of the green, particularly if it is a flat green. If you have a slower green you want to naturally use a different club and aim for the middle of the green. You will also need to factor in clean grooves, a better ball and good contact between the two that will result in a solid contact in which you can introduce a level of control on what the ball does when it lands on the green. Sadly, some days the green will be hard and other days it will be soft and this also will affect the reaction of the ball when it hits the putting surface. We are not looking for you to fly 10 yards past the flag and then back spin to the hole for a simple tap in. We have to be realistic here. However keeping those clubs clean and using new balls will work wonders to you being able to FIND the green and most importantly STAY on it.

Try This As Well:

If you're practicing, try this strategy and I would honestly suggest doing this out on the course where you can measure real feedback:

If you're at 200 yards out try using a 4 or 5 iron, take 5

shots with each club after an appropriate amount of warming up. Then establish which one gets you to the 200 yard distance cleanly, with a little bit of rolling. That way you won't be so likely to shoot into a bunker, water hazard or into the woods. This leads us on to accuracy because we are talking on the verge of ideal shots where you only have to worry about distance. The reality is that amateur golfers in one way or another are plagued by the odd errant shot - the unwelcomed slice, hook or the dreaded 'S' word – Shank. To remedy this I would suggest a lot of practice under the guided supervision of a teaching pro, or try to spend some time on YouTube learning the fundamentals of golf if you cannot afford lessons. Some of my other books address these issues; however a teaching pro would always be my first suggestion.

Playing it safe

You need to be realistic in your game. If you find the target more on shorter distances, and your putting is good, then it may not be a bad idea to play for example three 7 irons to a par 5 rather than a driver, 5 iron, and wedge. I recall a time when I forgot to put my woods back in my bag and I rushed to the course for a Saturday competition. I was shocked to see my bag with no woods in. It did force me to play it safe. And I tell you what; I played some of my best golf. I made par on every par 5, because I took all the hazards out of play. Sure, I didn't get any birdies but I taught myself a valuable lesson. Try it one day and I am convinced you will be surprised with the outcome.

7. Practice, Practice, Practice

How do you create a plan for more accurate shots in your short game? I would suggest you introduce some fun into your golf. You need to enjoy yourself and at the same time you can actually give yourself the best chance to get better. I used many different practice drills but these are four of my favorite. Sadly I cannot take credit for them, but after I was taught them during a course led by Dr Karl Morris I found them to be most beneficial. See what you think.

1. Different clubs, same distances:

In order to master your golf from within 120 yards you need to be able to get a hold on something Seve Ballesteros was well known for – FEEL. He would play on the beach in Spain with nothing but a 3 iron and developed an amazing ability to play a variety of shots with one club.

You can develop this too by using 1 club to play to a variety of different targets. One reason this is so helpful is because occasionally you will find yourself out of position – perhaps under a tree with low hanging branches. What will you do? You cannot power the ball with a Wedge hoping to find a gap in the branches despite everyone saying trees are 90% air. That just won't work. So a great way to practice feel is to use different clubs to the same distance

The aim of this drill is to allow your instincts to dictate how far the target is in your mind and then put the swing on the club that will get the ball to the intended target.

On occasion you will also have to play in adverse weather conditions and may need to play the ball under the wind. In cases such as this it would be better to take a smaller swing with a longer iron and control the roll out of the ball than try to fly the ball to the flag with a pure pitch shot.

On the reverse of this drill I would also suggest using one club to different distances.

1. Start at 125 yards and hit one ball to the target
2. Move to 115 and use the same club to hit to that same target
3. Move to 105 and change to whatever club you hit from this distance
4. Move to 95 and hit the same club as you did from 105
5. Move to 85 and hit whatever club you would from this distance
6. Finish by hitting your 85 yard club from the 75 yard position.

Some players choke down on the club and change their ball position for distance control and others use swing length and tempo. Experiment with both and see what works for you.

2. Virtual Reality Practice

I speak about this philosophy in my other book 'Break 80' and it is one of the best game/practice drills you can introduce. It centers on the effectiveness of your practice. When we think of Virtual Reality we think of films such as the 'Lawn Mower Man' and other headset wearing games. Think too about a pilot learning to fly. HE will use a simulator. It's not real, its virtually real, but it puts them in the best place to practice so that they do not crash a million dollar Boeing 747. He reason I mention Virtual Reality in the sense on your golf is that your practice need to mimic real life situations but not in a competitive setting. This is hard to appreciate but it entails on going out to the golf course rather than the driving range and playing shot after shot that you are likely to face. I would also minimize the amount of shots your play to half a dozen or so. This forces you to focus on the job at hand an train the mind to link to the body in these situation so that you are better prepared for the real thing in a competitive situation. You could do this in and around the chipping green too.

3. Holing chip shots

This is great drill for improving your chipping quickly and works on channeling your focus to help you appreciate that getting up and down is easy if you have the goal of chipping in to start with.

1. From the edge of the green, pick a hole on the practice green that's about 20-25 feet away.
2. Take your 6-iron and go through your pre-shot routine
3. Part of your pre-shot routine needs to see a) the ball coming off the face of the club and b) rolling into the hole. Don't worry if this is not the outcome as we are simply getting ourselves in the correct frame of mind to ACCEPT the outcome we are looking to achieve.
4. I then want you to practice holing out. When you have holed out I would like you to repeat the process at 15 feet and then 5 feet.
5. Feel free to have some fun with different slopes to the holes. After doing this for 30 minutes and holing a number of putts your confidence will be on a whole new level as you will approach chip shots with a degree of

expectancy which should focus you and lead to a maximum two putt with enough practice.

4. Par 18 game for the Short Game

This game was devised by Mind coach, Karl Morris.

1. From around the green, you're going to pick 9 locations to play from, 3 easy, 3 medium and 3 difficult.
2. Each mini hole is a par 2 and by playing all 9 holes your make the total "Par 18"
3. Play all 9 holes and keep your score and make 18 your target.

This is such a great game an goes hand in hand with practice routine number 3.

8. Pre-Round Warm Up to Sharpen your Short Game

So we may not possess the skills of Rory, Phil, Bubba or Jordan Spieth, but one thing a lot of golfers don't realize is that you can use part of their short game warm up strategy in your game. Yes, these players all have a rock solid pre-round warm up that is the same over and over again. They wouldn't be where they are today if they didn't.

Think about this; what if you just used 10 to 20 percent of their warm up tips before a round, how much better would your game would be? I think it would -as long as you take action on it regularly. It is possible. Having a short pre-round short game practice session will keep you on track and you will want to make it a habit. A good habit I think.

Set Up Near The Practice Green:

Before we even do this part, get to the course a little earlier than usual so you can spend sufficient time at the short game practice area. Maybe a half hour to an hour before if you can. Try to make it a priority to allow even 5-10 minutes at least. How many of us start to play good golf after 4 or 5 holes when we tell our playing partners that we have found a rhythm now.

Okay, there is no need to be fancy here just find a routine that works for you.

1. Start by draining some 2 to 4 foot short putts. Hit about 10. Don't worry about sinking all of them.
2. Next you want to drain some longer putts of 5 to 10 feet. Don't worry about perfection or using one hand. Those are advanced techniques. Even the pros would say to keep it simple even if you're a top amateur or pro.

Focus your putting on the shorter putts, because that's where your game gets tougher. One thing I like to do is practice with 1 ball rather than hit ball after ball from the same spot on the green. I am looking to simulate a real situation where I would only have the one ball on the golf course.

Do that short putting practice for about 5 to 8 minutes. The best short putting sessions are short, intense and doing them regularly will help your game big time!

Time to Move Over to Some Pitch and Wedge Shots:

Like I said, keep your short game warm up before a round short and sweet. No need to do long drawn out practice sessions before a game. You are looking to warm up and find your rhythm and timing.

Most courses have a short game area. Typically the chipping green will not be the same one as the main practice putting green. You may even have a driving ranging or at the very least a driving net. All courses are different. Just check with the course before you go practicing before a game. It's that "good old golf etiquette thing again."

50 Yard Pitches:

Don't try to do extremely long pitch and wedge shots, because you're doing a short game warm up. Not a mid-range or long game warm up. What you want to do here depending on the practice area is set up about 50 to 60 yards from the green and practice getting your pitch and wedge shots to the green, that's it. Don't do any Hail-Mary shots. We're not attempting to make up for lost strokes.

That's the way you have to think about your short game

actually, as if you haven't lost any shots. Jack Nicklaus always said that you can't worry about your last shot. Just move on to the next one.

As well, move the ball so you're targeting different areas on the green with your wedge and pitch shots. Kind of simulating real game situations you might be in. Your wedge and pitch shots will get better if you do this believe me. Don't worry about putting your ball in the rough, a sand trap or the woods; because all that will do is frustrate you.

You just want to get in some solid wedge and pitch shots along with your short putts.

You'll want to include this little tidbit short game wise as well...

Remember the short game tip I gave you if you're just at fringe of the green.

This tip is for those of you who have a tough time using a wedge at the green fringe. I said to actually use a putter so you get a better roll and your ball stays on target more effectively. Use this tip to get the ball closer to the cup. A wedge club is actually tough to use if you're not used to the loft on it.

It's more for shots from 50 yards and beyond.

Going back to pitch and putt shots. Combine both pitch shots from 50 to 60 yards out, then for the balls that land near the green fringe, use your putter and take some solid shots to get the ball closer to the cup. Don't worry about holing those putts from the fringe, because it's more important to get that pre-short game warm up in more than anything else.

Use that pitch and putt method fully when you're practicing at other times when you don't have a scheduled game with your golf buddies.

Now, for the warm up tip with your pitch shots and putts at the green fringe, do about 10 of each. Because you're doing two shots in one and doing both of them will take approximately 10 minutes if worked correctly. The same bodes for your short putts.

A good short game warm up will last about 20 minutes at most. It's not a marathon. It's about focused short game practice that combines pitch and putt shots. And remember to keep the pitch and wedge shots to 50 or 60 yards out and move the ball around the fairway to target different areas on the green.

That way when a pitch shot bounces off the green you'll make a note of that and practice that in your pre-game warm up, and in your regular short game practice sessions.

I like to make it simple guys. Try this out and make a commitment to it.

9. Putting Tips and Principles to Strengthen Your Short Game

Okay guys congratulations if you've made it this far in reading and taking action on every chapter of making your short game what it should be. It takes educating yourself, learning from pros and then taking decisive and consistent action to do it. And the same bodes for your putting which we will get to in a moment.

You're dedicated golfers and I want you to succeed. Not to show up your old golf buddy who bragged when he beat you all the time, but to get better and show yourself you can become a great golfer who could possibly compete for a Q-School card, or be a great local amateur. Who knows?

What do you think you should know though before you even start putting on greens? What's important to know? Well first of all most putts are short ones, well 40 to 50% of putts are anyway. Just the way it is, and you need to start focusing on that.

That's why it's imperative to practice your long putts, pitch and chip shots constantly so you're getting those shots closer to the hole, and doing them in fewer strokes.

Putter Club Head Angle:

That may seem contradictory but keeping your putter club head square to the target is more important than where the putter path is. As long as the club head is square to where the target is, then even if the putter path is off line a bit it won't matter much. That unorthodox swing comes into play again.

This all means that perfection of putting is not needed. Just a few basic principles like keeping the putter club head face square is more important than the putter, or putting path or even your mechanics to some degree.

How to Minimize 3, 4 or Even 5 Putt Holes:

It's not fun I know, but getting your long putts of 30 to 40 feet close is essential to preventing going beyond 3 putting a hole. Here's a tip believe it or not I thought of myself. Most teachers say you need to get your long putts within 5 or 6 feet of the hole, but they don't really go into how to do that a lot. It's not so much an issue of mechanics and keeping your putter in line to the shot, but I think it's a question of putt speed.

Think about it, you see a lot of lag putts where the pro

golfer falls short of the hole by more than 5 or 6 feet and end ups with a 4 or 5 stroke hole. No fun at all.

Here's what to do. Keep your mechanics in mind and practice your putting speed through your putting swing on those long 30 to 40 footers from the fringe of the green. Literally practice those shots to see how close you come to the hole. If you can get it within 5 to 6 feet regularly, you're doing well.

Remember the pre-round short game practice tips I gave you? I talked about using your putter from the fringe of the green. But I didn't talk about how close to get it to the hole.

Practice your putt speed on these long putts from 30 to 40 feet guys. That way you will 3-putt at most. Simplicity in golf is best.

Also, do not just practice your putt speed in getting it as close as you can to the hole, putt it past the hole as well and see how you do by varying putter speed in your shots. That will give you a different perspective and approach on it, because you may play a better putt beyond the hole depending on the lie of the green. I tried this myself when I was coming up 8 feet short of the hole for along time. I started hitting the ball much harder and end up about 4 foot past the hole. It was a psychological change. I was scared of hitting it past the hole, but in effect hitting it short 8 feet I had 12 feet to play with by going 4 feet past the hole. This is because when we see a putt we want to get it in the hole or apply the brakes just before the hole for a tap in. This causes us to hold back, especially if we are worried about a longer putt. Can you think of a time when you have hit a firm putt that has raced towards the hole and as we put our heads in our hands we see it end up just two to three feet past the hole. What would you rather have? A confident stroke that goes a couple of feet too long or a timid putt which we quit on that ends up six to eight feet short?

Here's another tip on putting. Vary your putter speed and the length of the back swing to get a handle on both distance of your putt and the speed it goes. Make sure your putting back swing is the same length as the follow through.

Basic Putting Strategy for Long and Short Putts:

Off the course I recommend practicing long and short putts 20 minutes a session. I find most people if they try to practice golf 45 minutes to an hour 4 times a week, never stick with it. That's why practice sessions of 15 to 20 minutes 3 or 4 times a week work well for busy people who love golf.

Try this out.

- 10 minutes of short putts from 2 to 10 feet from differing angles, lies and green conditions.
- 10 minutes of long putts from 10 to 40 feet from differing angles, lies and green conditions.

Include a short session on getting your putting speed and distance control down, from both short and long distance's as well.

You don't need one hour practice sessions. If you were an advanced amateur or pro I would advise it, but even they do short 20 to 30 minute sessions twice a day. Some do twice that a day. But doing more and more won't necessarily mean becoming better.

Keep these things in mind when putting and your short game will get better. Putting well, along with your mid-range chip and wedge shots are the key to your game, and your short game especially. So take the time to practice all this lovely stuff in the golf game we love so much.

10. Conclusion

Why It's Vital To Your Whole Game, and An Overview On These Tips So You Take Massive Action To Become A Short Game Guru!

Lowering your scores can be a daunting task even when you've been shooting over 80 or 90 on average for months if not years. Your putting is off, your pitching needs work or your long drives have been for the birds lately. From this 10 chapter program on getting your short game on track we delved into how to emulate the pros in their short game, and how to even use just a smidge of their putting and pitching acumen to accelerate your short game to levels you never dreamed possible before you came across this short game course.

You may not think it's important to know, but keeping track and taking down your short game stats,   not just if you're putting or pitching from certain distances, but where these shots are landing, and even keeping track if you're not doing well. That will give you golden nuggets of info on what to practice on more in your short game.

Think about this...

Your long game might be spectacular, but your short game

might be horrendous. So when your drives land at say 250 yards, calculate how far you drive it and where to. Use an app or GPS device to calculate how far you're hitting the ball.

Keeping stats on the shots you do well, and aren't doing well with, will help you stay driven to do better in your game.

Ahhh—the Secret of 120 Yards...

This is probably the key to your game. You may still be using a driver or wood at the 120 yard mark, but if you're using an iron or wood you want to determine the "lay of the land" on the green and if it's more flat, or down slope's a bit. That way you can figure out if you need to back off on your shot from 120, or more of a full swing is warranted.

That way you can make a better shot to the green or just close enough to get a pitch shot in close to the hole. You'd almost think this last part was more training. But I'm all about giving golfers massive value. Knowing your short game stats and how best to approach your game from 120 to even 100 yards is the absolute key to success in your game. Not driving the ball 300 yards. It might get you closer, but if your short game is "terrible" you will always have lingering issues with your pitch and putt shots. You might even have issues with iron shots from 120 even if your driving is incredible!

I'm not trying to make this more difficult, I'm making it so you're always prepared guys. That way you don't go into a mental state that says you can't do it. I know you can if you're prepared.

And we talked about the dreaded sand trap and how to use those tips from what I called "The Sand Trap Explosion Shot" using your pitching wedge just so you would make those shots easier. And it's not about hitting the ball on top of it either like you might think. It's the other way around. Who knew?

We went into the 5 key shots to take with your wedges, and how to use them properly to get your shots closer, and in an advantageous spot on the green to sink those easy putts like clockwork. It's not all peaches and cream but in golf as other sports mistakes are part of the game, and developing strong mental toughness is key even in the face of major mistakes in your game, so you can use these tactical tips in your short game to come out on top.

Missed greens are another issue that doesn't get talked about much either.

This is overlooked by a lot of golfers and even teachers to some degree. What clubs or pitching wedges are working well to get you on the green, or even going past the green. And remember our tip on practicing pitch shots to different areas on the green to give you more leverage when you eventually putt. Yes, I'm a geek and nut bar for this stuff but I believe in helping golfers and sports lovers like you guys.

When it comes to getting the ball to the green with an effective pitch shot you always want to think about where you want it to land, and get your results in advance by practicing those shots. You may not always be able to get the pitch shot to the green under par, but having a longer approach can sometimes work to your benefit so you're not going too far over par for a hole.

Practice Routines

They really can be fun but require discipline which can be difficult when most of us just want to have fun. But if you want to excel at golf you need discipline, and a practice routine for your short game will always keep you ahead in the game. It's almost like having money in the bank. The pros think like that, and even if they win only one out of 20 tournaments a year, and are coming in the top 20 to 40 most tournaments - they're doing well.

But having a strong short game is still important, so practice your short game from 120 yards and in with pitch shots, and not just from the same kind of lies and fairway conditions. You want to practice from sand traps and the rough as well. That way when those shots do come up, you'll be more prepared—and have the mental toughness to deal with it head on.

Even having a short pre-round practice session can get you psyched up for your game. Don't try unbearably difficult shots, do the ones from 100 to 120 yards and in. 10 pitch shots from 50 to 75 yards at most, and if you've been practicing them away from the course you'll be sure to hit it solid when you get to the course for real. Remember, you do not have to fear hitting all 18 greens. By now you should have a different level of confidence about your short game in getting up and down. And this is key because it suddenly makes missing a green no so much of a problem, and now all of a sudden the target is that much bigger from the middle of the fairway.

Having a comprehensive putting routine of long putts from the green fringe and along with that focusing in on both short putt and long putts with keep you in the game you love. But keep this in mind as well. When practicing putting, you have to start from literally tap in putts and work yourself up to 5, 10 and 20 feet putts all the way to the green fringe. It's about slow progression, it's not a race guys. You'll enjoy your game more if you take your time, learn slowly, be prepared mentally for mistakes and learn how to combine both pitch and putt shots in your short game from a practice and pre round perspective. Then do short regular effective practice sessions that keep you engaged and learn from the data you produce. Oh, and remember to use that putter from the green fringe if you're not so confident or adept with a pitch wedge. 'Works like a charm."

So that's it. If you haven't done so already get started and use these scoring zone tactics to skyrocket your short game where you know it deserves to be.

I wish you so much success on the course and in your short game. As always I would love to hear from you at info@confidentgolfer.com and if you liked this book I would be so grateful if you left a review. Take care and keep swinging the club.

Made in United States
Orlando, FL
18 March 2023

31143478R00050